Water

Guided/Group Reading Notes
Purple Band

Contents

OXFORD

Introduction

Reading progression in Year 2/Primary 3

In Year 2/P3, children begin to read independently.
They use longer texts containing both familiar words
and unfamiliar words that are not completely decodable.

The books at **purple band** are slightly longer than those at turquoise
band, but they still contain a core of high and medium frequency
words and phonetically regular words, which support children as they
build reading confidence and fluency. New vocabulary is introduced
within the context of familiar words, and dialogue develops
characterization. Descriptive vocabulary is used, e.g. *skimmed* and
dipped in *Don't Look Down*. Natural-sounding language is
employed throughout the books. This encourages readers to use
their knowledge of the rhythms and structures of language to
make sense of the text.

The complexity of character, plot and setting continues to develop,
giving many opportunities for inference, deduction, drawing
conclusions, and recall. Readers encounter both compound and complex
sentences, but there is still a wide range of simple sentences. A range
of punctuation is used including speech marks and apostrophes (both
contraction and possession).

A range of non-fiction features including charts, maps, instructions,
labelled diagrams, captions, indexes and glossaries are used to
encourage children to read and interpret information presented in
a variety of ways.

Visual literacy is supported through additional information in the
illustrations and photographs. Specific suggestions for comprehension
strategies associated with visualization and other sensory
interpretations are provided.

Progression in the Project X character books

This cluster contains a two-part story. In *A Wild Ride*, the children decide to build a micro-raft following a heavy rain shower, They have an exciting ride until it gets out of control. The raft breaks apart and Ant is washed up on an island in the middle of a pond. The reader is left with a cliffhanger ending. The story is continued in *Don't Look Down* where Max, Cat and Tiger have to think of a way to rescue Ant.

These stories continue to build the readers' understanding of the powers of the watches and the personal characteristics of Max, Cat, Ant and Tiger.

Guided/Group Reading

The engaging content and careful levelling of Project X books makes them ideal for use in guided/group reading sessions. The advantages of using guided/group reading, as well as charts to help you assess the appropriate level for a reading group, are outlined in the *Teaching Handbook* for Year 2/P3.

To use the books in guided/group reading sessions, you should select a level that creates a small degree of challenge for the group. Typically, children should be able to read about 90% of the book unaided. The level of readability enables them to practise their reading and build reading confidence, while the challenge provides opportunities for explicitly teaching reading skills.

These *Guided/Group Reading Notes* provide support for each book in the cluster, along with suggestions for follow-up activities. At purple band, the set of notes for each book could form one or two guided/group reading sessions.

Speaking, listening and drama

Talk is crucial to learning. Children need plenty of opportunities to express their ideas through discussion and drama, and to listen to and watch the ideas of others. These activities build reading engagement, personal response and understanding. Suggestions for speaking, listening and drama are therefore provided for each book.

Within these *Guided/Group Reading Notes*, the speaking and listening activities are linked to the reading assessment focuses.

Building comprehension

Understanding what we have read is at the heart of reading. To help readers become effective in understanding a piece of text, these *Guided/Group Reading Notes* contain practical strategies to develop the following important aspects of comprehension:

- Previewing
- Predicting
- Activating and building prior knowledge
- Questioning
- Visualizing and other sensory responses
- Deducing, inferring and drawing conclusions

- Determining importance
- Synthesizing
- Empathizing
- Summarizing
- Recalling
- Personal response, (including adopting a critical stance).

The research basis and rationale for focusing on these aspects of comprehension is given in the *Teaching Handbook* for Year 2/P3.

Reading fluency

Reading fluency combines automatic word recognition and reading with pace and expression. Rereading, fluency and comprehension are linked together in a complex interrelationship, where each supports the other. This is discussed more fully in the *Teaching Handbook* for Year 2/P3.

Opportunities for reading aloud are important in building fluency, while reading aloud to children provides models for expressive, fluent reading. Suggestions for purposeful and enjoyable oral reading and rereading/re-listening activities are given in the follow-up sections of these *Guided/Group Reading Notes*, and in the notes for parents on the inside cover of each book.

The Project X *Interactive Stories* software can be used to provide a model of reading fluency for the whole class and/or opportunities for individuals or small groups of children to listen to stories again and again. Listening to stories being read is particularly effective with EAL children.

Building vocabulary

Explicit work on enriching vocabulary is important in building reading fluency and comprehension. Repeatedly encountering a word and its variants helps to build recognition on sight. The thematic 'cluster' structure of Project X supports this because words are repeated within and across the books. Suggestions for vocabulary work are included in these notes. The vocabulary chart on pages 10 and 11 shows when vocabulary is repeated and new words are introduced. It also indicates those words that can be used to support learning alongside a structured phonics and spelling programme.

Developing a thematic approach

Helping children to make links in their learning supports their development as learners. All the books in this cluster have a focus on **Water**. A chart showing the cross-curricular potential of this theme is given in the *Teaching Handbook* for Year 2/P3, along with a rationale for using thematic approaches. Some suggestions for cross-curricular activities are also given in these notes, in the follow-up suggestions for each book.

Hang on!

In guided/group reading sessions, you will want to encourage children to make connections between the books in the cluster. Grouping books into a cluster allows readers to make links between characters, events and actions across the books. This enables readers to gradually build complex understandings of characters, to give reasons why things happen and how characters may change and develop. It can help them recognize cause and effect. It helps children reflect on the skill of determining importance, as a minor incident or detail in one book may prove to have greater significance when considered across several books.

Note that the **Water** cluster contains a two-part story, told in *A Wild Ride* and *Don't Look Down*.

In the **Water** cluster, some of the suggested links that can be explored across the books include:

- building water-related vocabulary e.g. the children can collect 'water words' from each book and create a word wall (**Literacy**)
- becoming 'Water Wise': gathering information on the ways that water is used at home and around the world (**Geography, Science**)
- researching and exploring the local environment e.g. rivers, flooding, ponds, water life (**Geography, Science**).

Reading into writing

The Project X books serve as models and inspiration for children's writing. Suggestions for relevant, contextualized and interesting writing activities are given in the follow-up activities for each book. They include both short and longer writing opportunities. The activities cover a wide range of writing contexts so writers can develop an understanding of adapting their writing for different audiences and purposes.

The Project X *Interactive Stories* software contains a collection of 'clip art' assets from the character books – characters, settings and props – that children can use in their writing.

There are also a number of writing frames that can be downloaded and printed for pupils to use, or that pupils can write/type into directly to practise writing and ICT skills.

Selecting follow-up activities

These *Guided/Group Reading Notes* give many ideas for follow-up activities. Some of these can be completed within the reading session. Others are longer activities that will need to be worked on over a period of time. You will want to select those activities that are most appropriate for your pupils. It is not expected that you would complete all the suggested activities.

Home/school reading

Books used in a guided/group reading session can also be used in home/school reading programmes.

Before a guided/group reading session, the child could:

- read the first chapter or section of a book
- read a related book from the cluster to build background knowledge.

Following a guided/group reading session, the child could (at home):

- reread the book to build reading confidence and fluency
- read the next chapter or section in a longer book
- read a related book from the cluster.

Advice for parents on supporting their child with reading at home is given in the inside covers of individual books. Further advice about home/school reading partnerships is given in the *Teaching Handbook* for Year 2/P3.

Assessment

During guided/group reading sessions, teachers or teaching assistants should make ongoing assessments of individuals and the group. Reading targets are indicated for each book and you should assess against these. You will want to select just one or two targets at a time as the focus for the group. The same target can be appropriate for several literacy sessions or over several literacy sessions or over several texts.

Readers should be encouraged to self-assess and peer-assess against the target(s).

Further support for assessing pupils' progress is provided in the *Teaching Handbook* for Year 2/P3.

Continuous reading objectives and ongoing assessment

The following objectives will be supported in *every* guided/group reading session and are therefore a *continuous* focus for attention and assessment. These objectives are not listed in full for each book but as you listen to individual children reading you should undertake ongoing assessment against these decoding and encoding objectives:

- Read independently and with increasing fluency longer and less familiar texts **5.1**
- Know how to tackle unfamiliar words that are not completely decodable **5.3**
- Read and spell less common alternative graphemes including trigraphs **5.4**
- Read high and medium frequency words independently and automatically **5.5**

Further objectives are provided as a focus within the notes for each book.

Correlation to the specific objectives within the Scottish, Welsh and Northern Irish curricula are provided in the *Teaching Handbook* for Year 2/P3.

 ## Recording assessment

The assessment chart for the **Water** cluster is provided on page 46 of the *Teaching Handbook* for Year 2/P3.

 ## Diagnostic assessment

If you feel that an individual child is failing to make good progress or seems to have a specific problem with an aspect of reading you will want to undertake a more detailed assessment. Details of how to use running records for diagnostic assessment are given in the *Teaching Handbook* for Year 2/P3.

Vocabulary chart

At Year 2/P3, children should:

- read high and medium frequency words independently and automatically
- read and spell the following:
  - compound words and polysyllabic words
  - less common alternative graphemes
  - suffixes and prefixes.

NB There are too many common high frequency words in each book to list all examples. It is assumed that the first 100 words are well established by this stage. A selection is given from the final 200 words in the *300 common words in order of frequency* list. Examples only are given in each category.

A Wild Ride	**High frequency words**	suddenly, fun, window, through, river, shouted, water, three, something
	Phonetically regular compound and polysyllabic words	outside, acorn, current, skimming
	Alternative graphemes for the same phoneme	/ee/ (ee, ea) three, he, screamed
	Context vocabulary	helmet, gushed, splash, faster, life jackets, whoosh, whizzed, paddle, island, rapids
Don't Look Down	**High frequency words**	fish, green, something, fast, dog, thought, where, were
	Phonetically regular compound and polysyllabic words	shadow, flapping, whispered, passing, splashed, landed, followed, pockets
	Alternative graphemes for the same phoneme	/or/ (or, au, aw, ou, our) caught, saw, your, boring
	Context vocabulary	island, micro-copter, strapped, steer, dipped, crashed, skimmed, insects, frogspawn, mini-beasts, scientific

Atlantic Adventure	High frequency words	more, long, boat, good, fast, small, food, clothes, friends, things
	Phonetically regular compound and polysyllabic words	himself, sudden, breaking
	Alternative graphemes for the same phoneme, including trigraphs	/ur/ (ur, oo, er) journey, were
	Context vocabulary	world, record, Atlantic Ocean, record, breaking, mast, motor, sail, nautical, squall, cockpit, satellite, navigator
Sam's Flood Plan	High frequency words	animals, river, every, school, garden, door(s), because, everyone
	Phonetically regular compound and polysyllabic words	anyway, upstairs, important, reports, without
	Alternative graphemes for the same phoneme	/u/ (u, oo, o) flood, up, come
	Context vocabulary	endangered, worried, power supply, crawled, spread, sealed, wrecked, sensible, action
The Water Cycle	High frequency words	water, fast, animals, fish, every, cold, friends, sea, grow
	Phonetically regular compound and polysyllabic words	hillside, eventually, rainwater, treatment, toothpaste, otherwise
	Alternative graphemes for the same phoneme	/ai/ (ai, ay, a-e, ey) rain, day, make, they
	Context vocabulary	water cycle, soaked, germs, chemicals, stream, drain, gurgles, frozen, turbines, electricity, desert

A Wild Ride

BY TONY BRADMAN

About this book

This is the first part in a two-part story. It's a rainy day so the friends decide to make a raft. They get more than they bargained for when they take it for a ride and the raft becomes out of control. Readers are left with a cliffhanger ending and the story continues in *Don't Look Down*.

You will need

- *A Wild Ride board game* Photocopy Master 27, *Teaching Handbook* for Year 2/P3
- *Water words* Photocopy Master 31, *Teaching Handbook* for Year 2/P3

	Literacy Framework objective	Target and assessment focus
Speaking, listening, group interaction and drama	○ Work effectively in groups by ensuring that each group member takes a turn challenging, supporting and moving on **3.2**	○ We can work together in pairs **AF1**
Reading See also continous reading objectives listed on page 9.	○ Explore how particular words are used **7.5** ○ Engage with books through exploring and enacting interpretations **8.2**	○ We can identify why the author uses certain words and devices **AF5** ○ We can explore the book and interpret the information we find **AF3/AF6**

Before reading

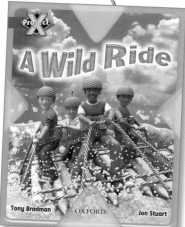

To activate prior knowledge and encourage prediction

- Look at the cover and ask the children to guess where the characters are. What is the weather like? How can they tell? (**deducing, inferring**)

- Look at the expressions on the faces of the characters. What do they think the characters are feeling? (**empathizing**)

- Ask them if they have ever been on a 'wild' ride. What was it like? What sort of wild ride do they think this story will be about?

- Discuss the sorts of activities that Max and his friends might do if it is too wet to go out and play.

To support decoding and word recognition and introduce new vocabulary

- Ask the children to look at the 'water words', e.g. *flowed, splashed* (p.6), *river* (p.7), *paddle* (p.8), *gushed* (p.11), *rapids* (p.13), *current* (p.16), *spray* (p.18). If necessary, help them decode the words. Discuss the meaning of the words and create a water-related word wall. The words can be written on paper leaves floating down the river, on fish swimming beneath the surface, or on water droplets from rain or a waterfall. Alternatively, you could use the *Water words* Photocopy Master. Continue to add any words that relate to the water theme as the children read this cluster of books, and encourage them to think of their own examples. (**previewing**)

- You may also wish to point out some of the high or medium frequency words, or practise decoding some of the phonically regular words in this book (see the vocabulary chart on page 10).

To engage readers and support fluent reading
- To build up tension, model how to read pages 2–5 with expression and clarity.

During reading

- Ask the children what they should do if they encounter a difficult word, modelling with an example from the book. Praise children who successfully decode unfamiliar words.
- Ask them to read to the end of the book.
- As they read, ask them to notice the 'water words' you have shared plus any other water-related vocabulary, e.g. *life jackets* (p.9).

> **Assessment point**
>
> Listen to individual children reading and make ongoing assessments on their decoding, sight vocabulary, strategies for tackling new words, and reading fluency. **AF1**

....>

After reading

Returning to the text

Ask:

- Why did the path look like a river to the micro-friends? (**activating prior knowledge, deducing, inferring**)
- Who had the idea of building their own raft? (**recalling**)
- How do you know when the friends are not enjoying themselves any more? What words do they use to express their feelings? (**inferring**)
- How do you think Ant is feeling at the end of this story? (**empathizing**)
- What do you think will happen to the friends in the next book? (**predicting**)

> **Assessment point**
>
> Do the children give coherent reasons for their views on the story? Do they need prompting to give an opinion or reason? How well do they express their opinions? **AF3/AF6**

....>

14

Building comprehension

- Ask the children to play the listening game 'telephone conversations' in pairs. This encourages the use of language rather than gesture. They should sit back to back with imaginary telephones for conversation. One person is Ant when he is stranded at the end of the book and the other is Cat. They should discuss how each of them is feeling and how Max, Cat and Tiger might be able to rescue Ant.
  (**empathizing**, **predicting**)

• ➔

Building vocabulary

- Discuss the author's use of capitals for whole words, e.g. *FUN!* (p.4), *SPLASH!* (pp.14, 16), *THREE!* (p.18). Why are these words in capitals?

> ### Assessment point
>
> Ask the children to feed back to their partner about their role-play games. Was the language clear? Did they remember all of the details? Did they build on each other's knowledge? Encourage the children to be positive and sensitive as they offer feedback. (Peer assessment) AF1

"We'll have to jump!" shouted Max.
The raft was now skimming across the grass. The air was filled with spray.
"On the count of three," yelled Max. "One ... two ... *THREE!*"

Max, Cat and Tiger jumped clear but Ant was too scared to let go. He clung on to the raft.
"*HELP!*" cried Ant.
"I can't look," said Cat.

- Why has the author used italics on page 4 when Max says "What's *that*?" Ask the children how it affects the way they read the text. How might they use the same techniques in their own writing?

Follow-up activities

Writing activities

- Write instructions for building a raft using the correct sentence and word level features, e.g. write in the imperative; in chronological order; use numbers or bullet points. (**longer writing task**)
- In pairs, complete and then play the *A Wild Ride board game* Photocopy Master based on the story. This activity is ideal for when it is too wet to go outside! (**short writing task**)

"Ant!" yelled Cat. "Are you OK?"
Ant got to his feet and waved.
"Phew!" said Max. "Now all we have to do is get him back."
Tiger looked around at the broken raft. "How are we going to do that, Max?" he said.

Cat looked out across the pond. Poor Ant seemed smaller than ever! Then she saw something move in the water. A giant shadow swam past.
"I think we need a bigger raft," said Cat …

To be continued …

Cross-curricular and thematic opportunities

- Investigate floating and sinking, e.g. which materials would be best to make a raft for children, or a life jacket, or a helmet? Which materials would not be suitable and why? Sort the materials into two groups. (**Science**)

- Compose a sound picture of *A Wild Ride* using tuned and untuned percussion instruments. Record the musical ideas using invented signs and symbols. Rehearse and perform the composition. (**Music**)

- Take digital photographs of the role-plays. Download the photographs into presentation software and ask the children to discuss what the actors were saying. They could add call outs as speech bubbles or compose a description underneath each photograph. They could also record dialogue to go with each slide. (**ICT**)

Don't Look Down

BY TONY BRADMAN

About this book

This is the second part in a two-part story, started in *A Wild Ride*. The children's raft has been smashed to bits and Ant is stuck on an island in the middle of a pond. Max and the others have to rescue him.

You will need

- *Dragonfly* Photocopy Master 28, *Teaching Handbook* for Year 2/P3
- *Dragonfly life cycle* Photocopy Master 29, *Teaching Handbook* for Year 2/P3

	Literacy Framework objective	Target and assessment focus
Speaking, listening, group interaction and drama	○ Speak with clarity and use appropriate intonation when reading and reciting texts 1.1	○ We can read a piece of text with expression **AF1**
Reading See also continuous reading objectives listed on page 9.	○ Explore how particular words are used 7.5 ○ Explain their reactions to texts, commenting on important aspects 8.3	○ We can identify why the author uses certain words and devices **AF5** ○ We can discuss what we think about a story **AF6**

Before reading

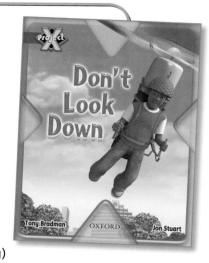

To activate prior knowledge and encourage prediction

● Look at the cover and ask the children if they can remember where the characters are and what the problem is. (**recalling, summarizing**)

● On page 3, the author says that Max, Cat and Tiger jumped *just in time*. What might have happened if they had stayed on the raft? Have you ever done something just in time? (**empathizing**)

● Have a book about freshwater life ready (or take the children to the school library). Discuss the different kinds of animals, especially insects, fish and amphibians, that live in or near a pond or stream. (**previewing**)

To support decoding and word recognition and introduce new vocabulary

● Ask the children to look at the 'water words', e.g. *stuck in the mud*, *huge drops of water*, *splashed* (p.8), *skimmed across the water* (p.13). If necessary, help children decode the words and discuss their meanings.

● If you have not already set up a water-related word wall, you could do so now. Otherwise, continue to add any water-related words and phrases to the word wall. Encourage the children to think of their own examples.

● You may also wish to point out some of the high or medium frequency words, or practise decoding some of the phonically regular words in this book (listed in the vocabulary chart on page 10).

To engage readers and support fluent reading

- Read page 4 aloud to the children, building the tension. Ask them what the author wants the reader to think has happened to Ant. They could take turns to read the page, emphasizing the suspense. How does the illustration help? (**predicting**)

 During reading

- Ask the children what they should do if they encounter a difficult word, modelling with an example from the book. Praise children who successfully decode unfamiliar words

- Pause at the end of page 5 and ask the children to compare the expressions of the children on this page with those on page 4. How does Cat know that Ant is OK? Ask them if they know of any other devices in books or films that show where the characters are. (**deducing, inferring**)

- Ask them to read to the end of the book. As they read, invite them to notice the 'water words' and phrases you have shared plus any other water-related vocabulary.

 After reading

Returning to the text

Ask:

- What are people able to do now that it has stopped raining (p.7)? (**activating prior knowledge**)

- Why does *gulped* (p.13) make you think of the huge fish as well as Max? (**visualizing**)
- Make a list of the wildlife seen by Max and Ant. (**recall**)
- Look at the text and illustrations on pages 15–17. How do the author and illustrator show that Ant is having a good time when Max finds him? (**empathizing**)
- Would you like to be a micro-explorer? (**personal response**)
- Do you think that the title of this book *Don't Look Down* works well? Can you explain why? (**personal response, adopting a critical stance**)

· ·>

Building comprehension

- Ask the children to play the listening game 'babble gabble' in pairs. After the initial reading, one child begins to retell the story to a partner as fast as he or she can, but with as much attention to detail as possible. After a minute, the teacher calls 'change' and the listener now has to continue with the story. This pattern continues for a number of turns. It is important to let the children know they do not have to tell the story in the same words as the book. However, they do have to listen carefully in order to remember the plot and sequence of events. (**recall**)

· ·>

Building vocabulary

- Point out the simile on page 9, *fast as a flea*. Why did the author use *flea* as a comparison and *jump* to show how Max hitched a ride with the dog? (Dogs have fleas that jump.)

- Discuss the use of the simile on page 12, *as wide as the ocean*.

- Ask the children to create similes of their own to describe the micro-copter, e.g. as light as a feather, as fast as a jet, as colourful as a dragonfly.

· >

Follow-up activities

Writing activities

- Develop the storyboard sequence (see the ICT task below) into 2–3 sentences per picture. (**short writing task**)

- Following the drama activity (see p.23), invite children to create a short descriptive writing piece describing in detail what it was like for Max in the mud and long, wet grass on pages 8–9. They could try to include figurative language. (**longer writing task**)

- Ask the children to imagine having a ride in a micro-copter. Challenge them to list the things they might see in their playground and school. What might they see from they sky that they can't see from the ground? (**short writing task**)

- Challenge the children to write an adventure based on a ride in a micro-copter. What device would they use to shrink to the right size in order to use the micro-copter? Where would they fly? Would they have an adventure or just enjoy the flight? Would they collect samples like the ones Ant left behind? Would they use the micro-copter to trick their friends and family? (**longer writing task**)

Other literacy activities

- In groups, act out what happens on page 8, e.g. move like Max in the mud, duck around the grass, swerve to avoid being stepped on by the dog. (**Drama**)
- Use the six pictures on page 24 to retell the story orally. Give one sentence per picture. (**Speaking and listening**)

Cross-curricular and thematic opportunities

- Label the parts of a dragonfly using the *Dragonfly* Photocopy Master. Illustrate a dragonfly's life cycle using the *Dragonfly life cycle* Photocopy Master. (**Science**)

- If possible, the children could find out about pond life in the local environment. (**Science**)
- Create sound effects for the micro-copter's journey using tuned and untuned percussion instruments, emphasizing specific danger points. (**Music**)
- Create tableaux of parts of the story, e.g. the three children looking at the fish and Ant on the other side. Photographs could be taken and speech bubbles added. The children could record the dialogue and add it to the presentation. (**ICT**)

Atlantic Adventure

BY MICHAEL PERHAM AND ALEX LANE

About this book

This is a biography about Michael Perham, the youngest person to sail single-handedly across the Atlantic.

You will need

- *Welcome home* Photocopy Master 30, *Teaching Handbook* for Year 2/P3

	Literacy Framework objective	**Target and assessment focus**
Speaking, listening, group interaction and drama	○ Explain ideas and processes using imaginative and adventurous vocabulary **1.3**	○ We can retell/continue a story using interesting words and phrases **AF2**
Reading See also continuous reading objectives listed on page 9.	○ Explain organizational features of texts **7.3** ○ Engage with books through exploring and enacting interpretations **8.2**	○ We can recognize how factual information is presented in a book **AF4** ○ We can explore a book and interpret information we find **AF3**

Before reading

- Ask, what does the title suggest the book might be about? Will it be fiction or non-fiction? What evidence do the children have for their opinions? (**deducing**, **inferring**)

To preview the text

- Look at the contents page and then at pages 2 and 3. Encourage the children to find the micro-friends and read their speech bubbles. Draw attention to the map and ask them to locate Britain, the Atlantic Ocean, North and South America. Why does Cat think Michael is brave? (**inferring**)

- Looking back at the contents page, ask the children which chapters they would be most interested in reading. As they go on to look at those sections, ask them to think about the comments made by Cat and Tiger (as fully as they can). (**personal response**)

- You may also wish to point out some of the high or medium frequency words, or practise decoding some of the phonically regular words in this book (listed in the vocabulary chart on p.11).

To engage readers and support fluent reading

- Scan the text for words in bold and show the children how to use the glossary at the back of the book.

- Why is the font for Michael's blog different from the main text (e.g. p.3)?

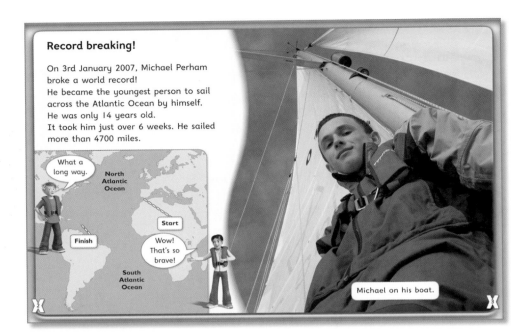

Record breaking!

On 3rd January 2007, Michael Perham broke a world record!
He became the youngest person to sail across the Atlantic Ocean by himself.
He was only 14 years old.
It took him just over 6 weeks. He sailed more than 4700 miles.

What a long way.

North Atlantic Ocean

Start

Finish

Wow! That's so brave!

South Atlantic Ocean

Michael on his boat.

 During reading

● Ask the children what they should do if they encounter a difficult word, modelling with an example from the book. Praise children who successfully decode unfamiliar words.

● Ask them to read to the end of page 7. Then look at pages 8 and 9 together, with a globe if possible, and discuss the route of Michael's journey. (**visualizing**)

● Ask them to choose a section from the contents page which appeals to them. (They may have time to read more than one, depending on the child.)

 After reading

Returning to the text

● Ask each child to tell the group which section they chose to read, why they chose it, and one interesting piece of information they discovered from their reading. (**recalling**)

- As you discuss each chosen section, ask the children how these pages differ from a story page (layout, information boxes, maps, photographs, glossary words in bold). (**building prior knowledge**)

....>

Building comprehension

- Working in pairs, ask the children to think of questions to ask the rest of the group. (**questioning**)
- Looking at pages 10 and 11, ask them to list the most important things Michael had to take with him. (**determining importance**)

....>

Building fluency

- Ask the children to find the extracts from Michael's blog throughout the book. Working in pairs, ask them to speak each section, concentrating on highlighting Michael's excitement.

....>

Building vocabulary

- Model the process of looking up a word in the glossary. Ask the children to return to the spread they selected and decide if any of the words not already in the glossary need explaining. If they do, work in pairs to compose glossary entries, using class dictionaries.

Assessment point
Can the children recognize how factual information is presented in a book? AF4

Assessment point
Can the children explore a book and interpret the information they find? AF3

Assessment point
Do the children speak with enthusiasm and excitement? AF2

- Check that they understand the purpose of the index. Are there any other words that they would like to be in the index?

Follow-up activities

Writing activities

- Ask the children to design a welcome home poster for Michael, using the *Welcome home* Photocopy Master. Encourage them to use the vocabulary which Michael himself used in his blog. (**short writing task**)

- Ask them to imagine that they are going to take a sea journey. They should write a diary or a blog of their adventures. As this is a story and not factual, there could be encounters with anyone, e.g. fantastic creatures or pirates. They could use ICT programs to write their story, adding illustrations and sound effects. (**longer writing task**)

What to see at sea

You might think that there is nothing to look at at sea. But Michael saw lots of things …

Extract from Michael's blog: 4th December, 2006

Had a fantastic display of dolphins before sunset. They must have been with the boat for at least 2 hours. They were jumping up in the air and being crazy. One dolphin made a huge jump out of the top of a wave. It was amazing.

dolphin

Michael took this photo of a dolphin from his boat.

Extract from Michael's blog: 16th December, 2006

Another flying fish jumped into the **cockpit** today. My dad said he saw a great long shark following him when we were drifting around. It was about 4 metres long! Scary stuff. I'm glad that didn't jump into my cockpit!

Cross-curricular and thematic opportunities

- The children could find out about Ellen MacArthur, when and where she sailed. (**Geography, History**)

- They could create a 3D display of sailing boats. (**Art and Design**)

- They could discuss how Michael could raise funds for his round-the-world trip and check his website. (**Mathematics**)

- They could listen to some music depicting the sea, e.g. Fingal's Cave, Scherezade, and then compose their own sea music (calm and stormy). They could record the musical ideas using invented signs and symbols, and rehearse and perform the compositions. (**Music**)

- They could create a sea scene using a variety of materials and processes after studying an artist who has produced seascapes. (**Art and Design**)

- They could use ICT programs to design a sailing boat. (**ICT, DT, Mathematics**)

Sam's Flood Plan

BY SIMON CHESHIRE

About this book

Sam is a boy who worries about everything, including flooding. He creates a flood plan, with instructions about what to do in a flood. When his street does flood, Sam's flood plan saves the day.

You will need

- *Water words* Photocopy Master 31, *Teaching Handbook* for Year 2/P3

	Literacy Framework objective	**Target and assessment focus**
Speaking, listening, group interaction and drama	○ Tell real and imagined stories using the conventions of familiar story language **1.2**	○ We can retell a story **AF2**
Reading See also continuous reading objectives listed on page 9.	○ Give some reasons why things happen or characters change **7.2** ○ Explain their reactions to texts, commenting on important aspects **8.3**	○ We can explain how characters change **AF2/ AF3** ○ We can discuss what we think about the story **AF6**

Before reading

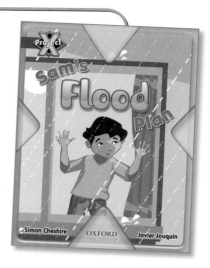

To activate prior knowledge and encourage prediction

- Look at the cover and ask the children to guess what the character is thinking and feeling. (**inferring**)

- Have the children experienced a flood or seen reports of flooding on the television? (**prior knowledge**)

- Ask if they can tell what the story might be about. (**predicting**)

- Discuss what might cause a flood.

To support decoding and word recognition and introduce new vocabulary

- Ask the children to tell you any examples of water-related vocabulary that they know. This could be from prior knowledge, or your previous discussions. Look at the 'water words' in this book, e.g. *river*, *flood* (p.4), *poured*, *rain*, *rained* (p.10), *leaks*, *trickled* (p.17) and add them to the *Water words* Photocopy Master.

- You may also wish to point out some of the high or medium frequency words, or practise decoding some of the phonically regular words in this book (listed in the vocabulary chart on page 11).

To engage readers and support fluent reading

- Ask the children to predict how Sam's character will influence what happens in the story. (**predicting**)

During reading

- Ask the children what they should do if they encounter a difficult word, modelling with an example from the book. Praise children who successfully decode unfamiliar words.
- Ask them to read to the end of the book.
- As you listen to individual children read, you might want to ask them to stop and summarize what has happened so far and predict what will happen next. (**summarizing, predicting**)

· ·>

One day, during the summer, the rain fell like water poured from a bucket. It rained and rained and didn't stop for days. The river began to rise.

"Don't worry, Sam," said Mum. "The rain will stop soon."

The rain didn't stop. The river rose. Water crawled slowly across the field. It spread out towards the houses.

Sam was very worried. He gave a copy of his flood plan to every house in the street.

After reading

- Look at page 3. Describe the kitchen. What can you see through the window? Does this illustration give you a hint as to what might happen in the story? (**predicting**)

- Sam worries a lot at the start of the book. Do you worry about the same things as he does? Why does he worry when it rains? (**empathizing, personal response**)

- You can see Sam's flood plan on page 7. Is this an easy plan to follow? What part of the plan could you help with? (**inferring, drawing conclusions**)

- On page 13, why does the illustrator give Sam a secret smile? (**inferring**)

• >

Assessment point

Can the children identify how Sam changes and why? **AF2/AF3**

- Look at the illustration of Sam on page 21 and compare it to the one on page 5. How does Sam's body language show the changes in how he is feeling? (**empathizing**)

- How did Sam face up to his worries about floods? Did his plan work? (**personal response, adopting a critical stance**)

• >

Assessment point

Do the children give a coherent reason for their views on the story? Do they need prompting to give an opinion or reason? How well do they express their opinions? **AF6**

Building comprehension

- Go round the group, asking them to retell the story using the illustrations on pages 22 and 23. Encourage them to use water-related vocabulary. (**recall**)

• >

Assessment point

Ask the children to feed back to each other. Was the language used clear? Did they remember all of the details? Did they build on each other's knowledge? Encourage them to be positive and sensitive as they offer feedback. (**Peer assessment**) **AF2**

Building vocabulary

- On page 10, the author describes the rain falling *like water poured from a bucket*. What does the author mean? Is this a little rain or a lot of rain? Have you read similes like this before?

- The author writes that the water *crawled slowly across the field*. (p.11) What sort of animal does the water seem to be behaving like? Does this make you feel more worried about what might happen to Sam?

Follow-up activities

Writing activities

- Ask the children to write instructions for Noah's flood plan. They should use the correct sentence and word level features, e.g: write in the imperative; in chronological order; use numbers or bullet points. Encourage the addition of humour, e.g. *Keep the mice away from the cats!* Use ICT programs to support the writing, adding illustrations and diagrams. (**short writing task**)

One of the things Sam worried about was the river. It ran across the field behind Sam's house. Sam was worried about the river rising and causing a flood.

He saw news reports on TV about floods. He saw streets and houses filled with muddy water. Nothing worried Sam more than that river. He worried every time it rained.

- Ask the children to write a picture book or use ICT programs to retell and illustrate a fairy tale involving a river (e.g. *The Three Billy Goats Gruff*, to be read to younger children). (**longer writing task**)

Cross-curricular and thematic opportunities

- They could ask parents and grandparents if the local area has ever been flooded. The information gathered could be put on a time line. (**History**)
- They could create a water scene using a variety of materials and processes after studying an artist who has produced water or river scenes, e.g. Monet. (**Art and Design**)
- They could create, perform and record a class composition using tuned and untuned instruments depicting a boat trip on a river (e.g: passing by a castle, under a bridge, through a tunnel, past a zoo) with the music representing the river as a recurring theme between each 'event'. (**Music**)
- They could use ICT programs to create a flood picture, exploring the shapes, colours and patterns of water. (**Art/ICT**)

The Water Cycle

BY STEVE PARKER

About this book

This book follows a raindrop character through the water cycle.

You will need

- *The journey of a water droplet* Photocopy Master 32, *Teaching Handbook* for Year 2/P3

	Literacy Framework objective	**Target and assessment focus**
Speaking, listening, group interaction and drama	○ Work effectively in groups by ensuring that each group member takes a turn challenging, supporting and moving on **3.2**	○ We can work together in a group to present our findings **AF3**
Reading See also continuous reading objectives listed on page 9.	○ Explain organisational features of texts **7.3** ○ Draw together ideas and information from across a whole text, using simple signposts in the text **7.1** ○ Engage with books through exploring and enacting interpretations **8.2**	○ We can recognize how factual information is presented in a book **AF4** ○ We can explore a book and interpret information we find **AF3**

Before reading

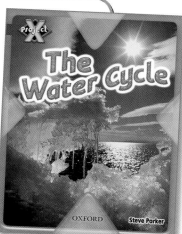

To activate prior knowledge and encourage prediction

● Look at the front cover. What do the children think a book with this title will be about? Look at the contents page. Were they right? Ask them to predict what each spread might be about. Which sections might give information or ideas that are new to them? (**previewing, predicting**)

● Working in pairs, ask the children to choose one section title. Discuss what they think it will be about. Then read the spread to confirm or amend predictions. Take feedback from around the group. (**predicting**)

● Find the index together. Select one entry and check where the reference leads.

To support decoding and word recognition and introduce new vocabulary

● Turn to the glossary. Ask the children to recap the purpose of a glossary and to compare it to the purpose of the contents page and index. Ask them to browse the book to find the words in bold that indicate a glossary entry. How do the explanations help them to understand the text more easily? (**questioning**)

● You may also wish to point out some of the high or medium frequency words, or practise decoding some of the phonically regular words in this book (listed in the vocabulary chart on page 11).

To engage readers and support fluent reading

● Read pages 2 and 3 together. What do the children think will be the role and purpose of the water droplet? Read the next two spreads together. Then ask them to read on to page 13. Ask them to tell the group about a new idea or fact that that they have learnt.

During reading

- Ask the children to read the rest of the book and find another new fact to share with the group when they have finished reading.
- Remind them what they should do if they encounter a difficult word, modelling with an example from the book. Praise children who can successfully decode unfamiliar words.
- Encourage them to check the glossary entries as they read.

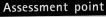

 ## After reading

Returning to the text

- The children should present their newly found facts to the rest of the group and be prepared to answer questions from the rest of the group. (**recalling, questioning**)
- Ask each child to prepare one question from their favourite section to ask the group. (**recalling, questioning**)
- As you discuss each chosen section, ask the children how the illustrations help the reader to understand the text. Which was the most interesting/informative photograph or illustration and why? (**giving a personal response, adopting a critical stance, visualizing**)

Building comprehension

● Ask the children to work in pairs to decide which was:
  ○ the most interesting place for the water droplet to be?
  ○ the most useful place to be?
  ○ the most unpleasant place to be?

  Remind them to use the contents page and index to help them make their decisions. (**determining importance, empathizing**)

● After discussions above, 'hot-seat' the water droplet. The children could take it in turns to answer questions about the water cycle in role as the water droplet. (**recalling, empathizing**)

Building fluency

● Demonstrate how to read pages 2–5 with appropriate pace and expression. Ask the children to read aloud round the group in pairs, a paragraph at a time.

Ice-cold water

It's now winter. The water is so cold, it cannot flow. It becomes hard and solid. This is called freezing. Frozen water is called ice. A sheet of ice freezes on the surface of the water.

Brr, I'm freezing!

In spring, when it is warmer, the ice will melt back into water. All of the river will flow again.

Follow-up activities

Writing activities

- Make a list of all the ways we use water at home and school. Use pages 10 and 11 to help. (**longer writing task**)
- Design a poster to show how we could save water in the home. (**short writing task**)

Other literacy activities

- Dramatize parts of the journey of the water droplet. (**drama**)

Cross curriculum and thematic opportunities

- After a class discussion, draw a plan of the journey of the water droplet in groups using the *The journey of a water droplet* Photocopy Master (i.e. raindrop, dinosaur, soil, stream etc.) (**Science/Geography**)
- Look at an atlas, a globe, ICT maps, etc to discover the major rivers and bodies of water (and deserts) in the world. (**Geography**)
- Research the animals and plants that are adapted to living with and/or without water. (**Science**)
- Make a 'Wonderful Water' presentation. Show all the activities you can do which rely on water in all its various forms, e.g: skiing in snow, playing at the beach, ice hockey, making a cup of tea. Use ICT programs to add photographs and sound. (**ICT**)